WRITE AROUND THE WORLD

WRITE AROUND THE WORLD

The story of how and why we learned to write

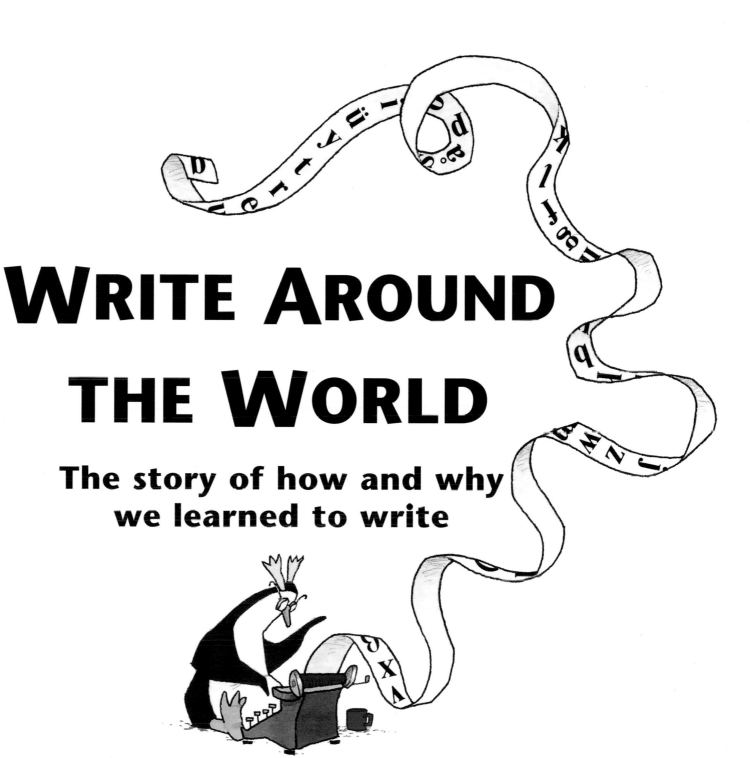

Vivian French & Ross Collins

How did it all start?

IN THE BEGINNING

OF THE BEGINNING OF THE BEGINNING

A CAVEWOMAN GRUNTED AT A CAVEMAN AND SPEECH BEGAN.

WE'VE BEEN TALKING EVER SINCE—

PROBABLY FOR MORE THAN 100,000 YEARS.

WE'VE BEEN USING LETTERS AND WRITING

FOR A MUCH SHORTER TIME.

PROBABLY ONLY ABOUT 6,000 YEARS.

As time went on the symbols changed.

To: The other farmer
Address: Sumeria
4000BC

3500BC
OX
BIRD

3250BC
OX
BIRD

IN SUMERIA

No one knows exactly how writing began, but it seems likely that people wrote numbers first. As far as we know, writing began in about 4000 BC in SUMERIA. The Sumerians were traders, which involved a lot of counting.

Maybe at first they counted on their fingers. Maybe they made nicks on a piece of wood. But the more developed their trade became, the harder it was to remember what they had agreed. Something had to be done about it. Records needed keeping.

Perhaps a Sumerian farmer sent another farmer a message to say "I'll trade you my ox for 5 hens," and to make it clear he drew pictures of 1 ox and 5 hens. The other farmer disagreed. He sent a message back, and because it took too long to keep drawing whole hens and whole oxen he made the pictures simpler and simpler, and **PICTOGRAMS** were invented.

CLAY and reeds were basic materials that everyone could get hold of, so writing on clay with a reed stick was the usual way to write. It was hard to make curves in wet clay, so the pictograms had lots of straight lines and wedge shapes (Δ). The word for wedge-shaped is CUNEIFORM.

Cuneiform writing had arrived!

3000BC

OX

BIRD

The first farmer
SUMERIA

IN CHINA

Meanwhile, on the other side of the world, similar things were happening. Did the idea of writing travel to China from Sumeria? Probably not, it is much more likely that the Chinese developed the idea without knowing what was going on in other countries. There is a legend that writing was discovered in China by 3 emperors about 28,000 years ago, and they wept and wailed all night long at the horror of it! Suppose EVERYBODY learned to read and write—they might discover that emperors weren't quite so very important after all. The first known examples of writing in China date from about 2,000 BC.

I'm an Emperor penguin!

女

As in Sumeria, pictures came first. And from pictures, pictograms developed.

SUN · MOUNTAIN · TREE

One pictogram—or **CHARACTER**—represented one idea or word. Gradually the old characters became more stylized and evolved into the characters still used in China today!

SUN · MOUNTAIN · TREE

There are many different languages spoken in China. The written language is based on Mandarin Chinese, and most people in China speak Mandarin. If you can read Mandarin you can read even the oldest writings—although it might take you a while to work it out. Maybe the emperors were right to be afraid!

IN EGYPT

In Egypt people were developing much more advanced pictograms than those used by the Sumerians. The new style of writing was called **HIEROGLYPHS**, a word meaning "sacred carvings." Many hieroglyphs were still easy to understand. But there was one huge difference.

Looks nothing like me ...

REED

WATER

OWL

Certain hieroglyphs could represent a single sound as well as a word—like the letters in an **ALPHABET**. And an alphabet offers a whole new way of writing!

The Egyptians began to write on **PAPYRUS**, the first ever paper. Using pens and papyrus meant writing was not limited to lines and wedges, and scribes could write much faster. But even with smooth papyrus, it was still difficult to write the hieroglyphs fast enough, so yet another form of writing developed, using simpler hieroglyphs. It looked much more like writing as we know it today and was called **HIERATIC**.

Faster! Faster!

This developed again into an even faster script, but then came the end of the Egyptian civilization. The Greeks invaded Egypt, and the scribes had to start all over again!

Learn Greek, scribe!

But I've only just learnt my hieroglyphs...

THE ALPHABET

If the Chinese had been international travelers when they were inventing their characters, more people might use their writing system today. But they weren't. The **PHOENICIANS** were though. They explored the Mediterranean and European coasts, and probably Africa. They were serious traders and in among their packages and bundles they packed their 22-letter alphabet—no vowels, only consonants.

Wherever they went, the Phoenicians brought their alphabet along. Phoenician doesn't use vowels much, but Greek does. So when they started using it, the Greeks added vowels.

The alphabet went traveling on. The **ETRUSCANS** borrowed the Greek alphabet and then altered it to suit themselves.

ETRURIA

ROME

THE REST OF EUROPE

←AMERICA

Pass it on!

Pass it on!

Pass it on!

10   PHOENICIANS   GREEKS   ETRUSCANS

When the alphabet reached Italy, the Romans nipped and tucked it to fit too.

An alphabet is such a brilliant idea. Some professors claim a child invented it! Instead of having to learn 20,000 pictograms, one for every word or idea, you can combine just 22 letters of the alphabet to make as many words as you like—even some you haven't seen or heard of before.

An alphabet is just the thing for a conquering army—flexible and light to carry.

So, as the Roman empire spread and spread, and the Romans marched all over Europe, they brought their alphabet along too.

How do we know about the alphabet's travels all across Europe? The Phoenicians didn't leave much writing behind them—maybe they were too busy trading to write poems and stories. We know much more about the ancient Egyptians and Greeks.

The earliest Greek **INSCRIPTION** dates from about 730 BC. This doesn't mean that they weren't writing before then, only that we have no proof of it. (Maybe all the pots got broken?)

GREECE

PHOENICIA

Take this!

A
B
C

ROMANS

THE REST OF EUROPE

11

A WORLD
OF ALPHABETS

As the alphabet moved, its use grew. As the Romans moved across Europe, people used the Roman alphabet to write down their own languages.

But different languages use different sounds, so people selected only the letters they needed. People who speak Irish don't use J, K, Q, V, W, X, Y, or Z—so they only need 18 letters!

As the Roman alphabet spread West, another family of alphabets was developing in the East.

ARAMAIC (also decended from the Phoenician alphabet) was the official **SCRIPT** of the Babylonian, Assyrian, and Persian empires. Like the Roman alphabet, Aramaic letters were used by many other peoples to write down their own languages.

Modern Hebrew, the script of the Jewish people, developed from Aramaic. So did **ARABIC,** and because it is the script of the Qu'ran, the sacred book of the Islamic religion, Arabic text is read by many people who don't speak the Arabic language!

Aramaic was used by traders and may have been taken to India, to develop into another family of alphabets!

But not all alphabets are old—the Native American script **CHEROKEE** wasn't invented until 1821.

What a great welcoming party!

All these alphabets are very different. They come in different lengths:

English uses 26 Roman letters, modern Hebrew has 22 letters, **KHMER** has 74, and the shortest is the Solomon Islanders' with only 11 letters! Their languages can be read in different directions: from left to right, like English, or right to left, like Urdu, or top to bottom, like Chinese, or even winding right to left, then left to right, every second linein what is called **BOUSTROPHEDON.**

All these people on the globe are saying welcome in their own languages and alphabets.

13

LANGUAGES

Suppose your friends from Jupiter landed here? They probably wouldn't understand WELCOME—whatever language you tried. What sign could you give instead? What about a smile? A smile is understood everywhere. But imagine if you read only Spanish, and you were sent messages in French or German. Would you understand them?

In medieval Europe people who could write knew about this problem. They found that even when everyone used the same Roman alphabet, the different languages made communicating a problem. So they decided to borrow something else from the Romans—their language, **LATIN.**

Because the Romans had conquered lots of countries, lots of people understood Latin. So the monks, scribes, and other people who could write began to use Latin for important communications.

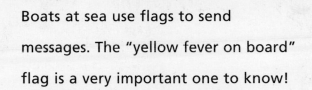

Latin is still used today, although not as much as before. Gravestones often have R.I.P. on them, which stands for *Requiescat in Pace*—or rest in peace. Latin is the international language of science. If you meet someone on the beach and you don't speak the same language, you'll still both know a Stegosaurus from a Tyrannosaurus Rex .

Plants have two names: a common name and a Latin name. Check out digitalis purpurea (foxglove)—it means purple finger!

You find Latin in medicine too—look at the names of the bones of a skeleton, like patella (kneecap).

ESPERANTO was invented to be the modern language that everyone could understand, but it hasn't quite made it! Can you speak it?

What other international ways of communicating are there? What about the international signs and symbols used in math and science? Anyone in the world will know "+" is plus—unless they don't know any symbols!

Morse code is international too. Groups of dots and longer dashes, either tapped out or flashed with light, signal different words.

Boats at sea use flags to send messages. The "yellow fever on board" flag is a very important one to know!

Can you read music? In the 17th century the Western **NOTATION** system was invented. Without it we wouldn't know what Mozart's music sounds like, because there weren't any compact discs back then.

HANDWRITING

BARGAINS!

Reed Sticks

Sandstone

Bamboo Brushes

Pen Cases

Inks

Papyrus

Paper

Reed Pens

Clay Tablets

The Sumerians wrote with sticks and clay, the Romans did it with **STYLUS** and wax tablet, the Chinese did it with pen and paper, the Egyptians did it with reed pen and papyrus.

Our ancestors did it, we do it. Writing is one of the most useful skills, whether you use a **QUILL** or a **COMPUTER.**

Handwriting changed to suit the materials and tools used. At first, the straight lines of capital letters were the easiest to write, but as materials improved these were soon overtaken by the script we have today.

Early writing was painstakingly slow work. If copies of documents were made it was always by hand. Often monks were scribes and they would

be employed by kings and queens to copy holy books, laws—or their favorite stories!

Because writing took so long, books were very valuable. In the **LIBRARIES** of Babylon and Egypt the books were chained up so no one could steal them. If you wanted a copy, you had to write it.

Some people say you can tell a person's personality from their handwriting, but if you think your writing is showing all the signs of belonging to an alien monster, don't worry!

Most people's handwriting doesn't settle down until they're 15 or so.

At the end of your letter you write your name. Everyone's signature is different.

Try writing your name in different ways. When you are famous, people will ask you for your autograph!

YOUR HANDWRITING ANALYSED

Tricky!

WRITE-U-LIKE

Sign here chum!

Parchment

Ink

Quills

Typewriter

Computer

Carbon Paper

Keyboard

Mouse

Goose Feathers

Pencils

Chalk

Fountain Pens

Ink

Erasers

ARTISTIC WRITING

Edna keeps practicing her autograph because she hopes to be a film star. She has heard that writing can be art. Is that her excuse for all this **GRAFFITI** in the art gallery?

What about you? How many times a day do you write your name? How do you write it? Any old way? Try decorating it and coloring it.

What about your initials?

Do you think famous people practice their autographs?

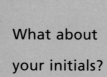

Ahem.

Decorative writing is called **CALLIGRAPHY**, and people have been doing it for a very long time. As far back as 2000 BC, scribes were making writing look nice as well as using it to communicate or record. This horse was done 400 years ago in Belgium.

Chinese writing has always been seen as an art form. Calligraphers still write today using brushes and ink even though Chinese text can be printed by machine. This is the character for "dragon."

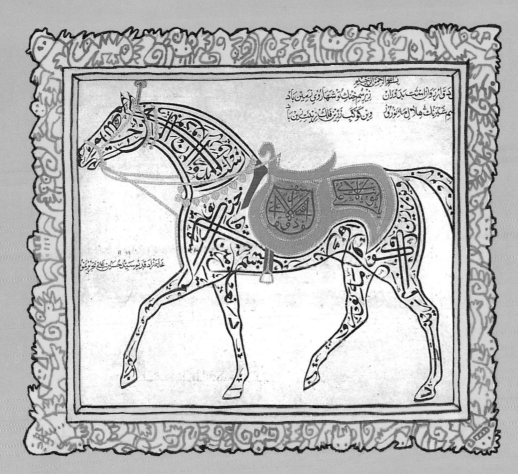

皇帝

Islamic tradition has precise rules about what can be shown in pictures, so the writers put all their effort into the letters. Islamic texts are some of the most beautiful in the world.

Writing can also be used to make a picture—a calligram. This rocket is made up of Latin words, meaning "Birds of a feather flock together!"

So, you can write, but suppose you've just written a very important message, and you want it read by hundreds of people. Are you going to write it out over and over again? Or get someone else to do it for you? Or (AHA!) invent a way of copying your message by machine?

Imagine if this book had to be handwritten and all the drawings colored in each time! It would cost hundreds of dollars for each copy.

As more and more people learned to read and write, more and more books were needed—and even the fastest writers couldn't make copies fast enough. (How quickly can you write—without making mistakes?!)

Although it became quicker to write when smaller, rounded letters came in, even this was not quick enough. Something more had to be done.

This is DE-PRESSING

20

The very first printed book may have been a prayer scroll made in 868 AD, in China. Each page was carved out of a wooden block and printed onto paper.

Printing came to Europe in the 15th century, introduced by Johannes Gutenberg, a German goldsmith.

He invented **MOVEABLE TYPE**—each letter was cast in metal, so it could be arranged in any order and could be used again and again. And, because a **PRINTING PRESS** can print thousands of copies at a time, books became much cheaper and easier to make.

To begin with, Gutenberg designed each letter to look as much like the letters written by German scribes as possible, so that the books would still look like handwritten books. The first ever typeface!

TYPEFACES AND PUNCTUATION

Express yourselves!

How can you tell one person from another? By looking at their face! Well, type can also have a face— a typeface. Typefaces have different names—often their names can give you a clue as to what they'll look like: Futura, **STENCIL,** Old English, Avant Garde.

If you smile, your face looks friendly. If you change your expression to a frown, your face looks fierce. Changing a typeface has the same effect—the feeling of the words alters. All type is carefully chosen to help present a message in the most appropriate way.

These days there are a huge number of different typefaces to choose from, and they can be accessed at the touch of a computer button.

New typefaces are constantly being invented—why not have a go at making one up yourself?

Even if the typeface gives you a hint of what the text is about and you understand the letters you might be a little confused if you did not find any punctuation punctuation helps to guide you so you know when to take a breath or else you might find you become purple in the face and have to lie down on the floor and puff very very hard.

We need more glue on the punctuation George!

If you read "no no no" you would not know how to read it. Is it frightened, is it forceful, is it a question?

no, no, no... **NO!!!** No?

Different languages use different punctuation. In English we recognize that something is a question when there is a sign like this "?" at the end of the sentence. In Spanish, this sign is placed at the beginning of the sentence as well—"upside down! *¿Como se llama?*—"What is your name?"

Many languages have **ACCENTS** which can completely change the **PRONUNCIATION**—and sometimes the meaning of the word itself. In Irish, *fear* means "man" but *féar* means "grass." Forgetting the accent could lead to confusion!

Punctuation is a code to help you read, pronounce, and understand writing.

23

SECRET CODES

Not all codes are intended to help you interpret information. Some are secret codes.

Why do we have codes, and when did they start? In the early days of writing, when only scholars and learned people could read and write, ordinary writing was a secret code to the many non-readers.

There is an ancient **NORSE** writing system called **RUNES**, and the word rune actually means secret.

The **RONGORONGO** script of Easter Island is still a secret and no one knows what it means!

Secret codes were needed urgently when more people knew how to read. Try this!

XIZ EJE UIF DIJDLFO DSPTT UIF SPBE?

Can you understand what is written here? It's written in a very simple code based on the letters of the alphabet.

Write the alphabet out twice, like this:

ABCDEFGHIJKLMNOPQRS...

BCDEFGHIJKLMNOPQRST...

Can you crack the code?

A=B, B=C, C=D, D=E, and so on.

Try your own code—move the second alphabet further along—and send a message to a friend. You can always include clues to help them, such as **A4,** which means that **A** is now four letters along, or **A=D**!

SLANG is also a form of code. Have you sometimes noticed that the language you use when talking to your friends seems not to mean anything to your parents? But remember, it's only a secret as long as your parents don't understand.

What about inventing your own secret word code— "It's raining bananas" could mean "Mom's in a bad mood!"

Sometimes **ACRONYMS** create mystery—what does **SoSoCo** mean? Easy— **SOciety for SOlving COdes!** and you and your friends are members now!

PICTOGRAMS ARE BACK!

Do you know what these signs mean? All of them—"no smoking," "elevator," "customs," and "lost and found" are found in airports. A set of 38 symbols was designed in the United States in the 1970s to help international travelers.

An enormous number of people travel all around the world and have to find their way around airports in many different countries. What happens if you don't speak the local language and you've lost your baby sister's teddy bear? Would you recognize the lost and found sign? Would someone who lives in a desert recognize it?

Could you design one that ANYONE could recognize?

OTHER SYMBOLS SHOW YOU HOW TO DO THINGS... OR HOW TO AVOID DOING THINGS!

Computers use symbols or signs called **ICONS**—or pictograms!

Just like the Sumerians did 6,000 years ago!

GLOSSARY

REED   WATER   OWL

ACCENT Many languages use accents to change the sound of the letter. Accents are acute as in café, grave as in pietà, circumflex as in tête, tilde as in señor, cedilla as in façade, or umlaut as in Köln.

ACRONYM A word made out of the first letters of a group of words, especially a long group: NASA stands for National Aeronautics and Space Administration.

ALPHABET A writing system that uses signs to represent sounds. The word comes from the two Greek letters "alpha" and "beta."

ARABIC has been written down since 1 AD and is studied by Muslims all over the world, whatever language they speak. If the Muslim Moors who conquered southern Spain in 756 had settled in the rest of Europe, Europeans might all be writing in Arabic today.

ARAMAIC developed in Aram (in what is now modern Syria) about 800 BC. It was used all over the Middle East and Asia Minor. Some of the Old Testament was written in Aramaic.

BOUSTROPHEDON means "like an ox plow." It is writing which runs from left to right— thgir neht—tfel ot thgir morf snur ti neht to left again—every second line!

CALLIGRAPHY This word comes from the Greek words "kallos" meaning "beautiful" and "graphein" meaning "to write."

CHARACTER The word used to describe the symbols used in Chinese writing. Some of the symbols can represent sounds, but only a tiny proportion in comparison to an alphabet.

CHEROKEE is spoken by the Cherokee people. The alphabet to write the language was invented in 1821 by a man named Sequoya.

CLAY was used widely by early people to make pots. The Sumerians began to use it to make tablets to write on. They wrote on the wet clay and then let the message dry.

COMPUTER from the Latin words "com" (together) and "putare" (reckon) or "add." It does calculations and stores information.

ESPERANTO Dr L. L. Zamenhof invented Esperanto in 1887. He hoped it would become a modern international language. In the beginning it was a success, it is estimated that 8 million people can speak it—but everyone would need to learn it for the idea to work.

ETRUSCANS lived in the west of central Italy between the 8th and 4th century BC. Their civilization was very sophisticated and they loved art. Many examples of their writing still exist, many of them on pots and jugs (like the one in the picture on page 10).

GRAFFITI This word was first used by archaeologists to describe informal writings on tombs. Now it is also used to describe any informal writing on a wall in a public space.

HIERATIC A simplified version of the Ancient Egyptian hieroglyphs, it became the everyday script from 3100 BC until 650 BC.

HIEROGLYPH An Ancient Egyptian picture or symbol used to represent an object or idea. Some could represent a sound (the "owl" sign above was also used for the sound "m") but they were only a tiny proportion.

ICON From the Greek word "eikon" meaning "picture." It is often used to describe the pictures/symbols used on computer screens.

INSCRIPTION Written words meant to last. The ancient Greeks sometimes painted inscriptions on their pottery.

KHMER The language of Cambodia.

LATIN was the official language of the Romans and later of science, medicine, and law. All Catholic masses used to be said in Latin so they were the same in every country.

LIBRARY from the Latin word *liber* meaning "book." The first library was probably the collection of clay tablets in Babylon in the 21st century BC. There were temple libraries in Egypt and Greece; sacred libraries in Jerusalem; monastic libraries in early Christian Europe; many Arabic religious and secular (or nonreligious) libraries; university libraries and national libraries like the Lenin Library in Russia and the Library of Congress in America. The first public library was in Greece in 330 BC, but free public libraries really developed in the United Kingdom and United States in the 1900s.

MOVEABLE TYPE was first invented by Bi Sheng in China. But because there are so many Chinese characters, it wasn't very useful. When Gutenberg used moveable type for the alphabet, it worked much better.

MANUSCRIPT from the Latin *manus* (hand) and *scriptum* (writing)—written by hand.

NORSE The language of the Vikings, who came from Scandinavia.

NOTATION The Western musical notation system has twelve notes. You have to learn them when you play an instrument.

PAPYRUS This grassy plant only grew in Egypt. It gave us our word for "paper."

PARCHMENT The skin of a goat, sheep, or other animal, cleaned for writing on.

PHOENICIANS developed the first alphabet. They lived in what is now called Lebanon and were the ancient world's greatest traders, particularly selling purple dye ("Phoenician" is from Greek meaning "trader in purple").

PICTOGRAM A picture or symbol representing an object, a word, or an idea.

PRINTING PRESS Gutenberg's printing press was inspired by a wine press. The moveable letters were arranged and covered with ink. Then paper was laid on top and pressed down.

PRONUNCIATION Even if you understand what a written word means, you still need to know how to pronounce—or say—it.

QUILL A feather used for writing. If you are right-handed you need a feather from a goose's left wing, and if you are left-handed you need one from a goose's right wing!

REEDS are tall stiff grasses that grow near water. They were in ready supply in Egypt, and the Egyptians used reed sticks as pens.

RONGORONGO means "chants" or "recitations" in the language of Easter Island. The detective on page 24 is trying to decipher it.

RUNES are ancient Scandinavian letters. The stones on the table in the picture on page 24 have runes on them.

SCRIPT is writing. It comes from the Latin word *scribere* meaning "to write." There are lots of other words related to it: scriptorium (a place for writing), scripture (sacred writing), manuscript, and scribe (a person who writes).

SLANG Made up words usually by someone trying to be diferent. Usually slang changes quickly and is trendy only for a short time.

STYLUS A thin stick of metal, bone, or ivory used for writing on wax tablets. It was more flexible than reeds and could do curves.

SUMERIA was an area where agriculture and trading flourished. It is the country where cuneiform was invented. The old name for the region was Mesoptamia which means "fertile crescent." It is now called Iraq.

Picture Credits and Acknowledgments

Page 19:
Victoria and Albert Picture Library
"Tugra," from North India, late C19

Chinese calligraphy for "Dragon"
by Manyee Wan
from Lao Lao of Dragon Mountain
Copyright © 1998 Zero to Ten Limited

Published in the United States by
OXFORD
UNIVERSITY PRESS
198 Madison Avenue
New York, New York 10016
www.oup.com

First published in Great Britain in 1998
by Zero to Ten Limited
46 Chalvey Road East, Slough, Berkshire SL1 2LR

A CIP catalog record for this book is available from
the Library of Congress.

ISBN 0-19-521924-4

Printed in Hong Kong

Vivian French worked in children's theater for ten years as both an actor and writer before turning to write children's books, and she has been writing and telling stories ever since. Vivian's published books are too numerous to mention, but highlights include *Caterpillar Caterpillar*, illustrated by Charlotte Voake, which was shortlisted for the 1993 Emil/Kurt Maschler Award, and *A Song for Little Toad*, which was shortlisted for the Smarties prize in 1995.

Ross Collins was born and grew up in Glasgow, graduating from the School of Art there. Since winning the Macmillan Prize for *The Sea Hole* in 1994, his work has been in great demand and he has been widely published in the United States and the United Kingdom.